ENGAGING HUMOR

How To Make People Laugh
Without Trying To Be Funny

V1.240711

MỤC LỤC

To celebrate my 10+ years of writing, I'm giving away three of my valuable books completely free of charge. All you have to do is to scan the QR or access the link below.

leorowan.com/qrhumour7

WHAT'S WORSE THAN GETTING HIT BY ONE BRICK?

You might be thinking the answer is... two bricks. Actually, the answer depends on what kind of brick it is and where it lands.

Over 15 years ago, I found my dream: becoming a great speaker. And soon, it became a nightmare, when I got hit by the bricks of doubt, and reality.

Every day, I dreamed of stepping onto a big stage, where I could make everyone laugh. I could imagine the loud clapping and the girls cheerings until I woke up. I was a shy guy. Talking to a girl was hard enough, let alone talking to a whole crowd of people.

And that's not the worst.

My parents, they worked in banking for years, spending lots of money for me to study finance at the best university. Can you imagine how they'd react when they found out about my dream?

I definitely need a helmet, a really hard one.

I'll never forget that dinner. Mom's soup was so sweet, dad's joke was so funny. Such a perfect chance to tell them my dream (and avoid some bricks). I took all of my courage and told them my dream of becoming a great speaker. Can you guess what happened?

Dad's face turned red, "Are you crazy?"

(Later, the one who actually went crazy was... him)

Mom just smiled, looking at me, as if to say, "A *great speaker? Does it have bluetooth?*"

The brick of doubt hit my heart.

You know, the stronger the love, the longer the pain. Sometimes, I wish that was a real brick, so the pain in my heart wouldn't last for years. "*Should I follow my impossible dream, or follow my parents' dream for a guaranteed job, and a guaranteed wife, who works in a bank, too?*"

Finally, I made my choice.

I worked as a copywriter at a big event company, with lots of great speakers. My boss, a serious man with gray hair, told me,

"To become one of our official speakers, you must have a special talent: Humor."

Yeah, I knew lots of jokes from my dad, maybe I could try, but I never had a chance.

Until one day, in a big event, hundreds of people clapped their hands, but the speaker was late... we needed to buy some time, and my boss, he panicked.

"*Wow, I could be the hero!*" I thought to myself, and walked onto the stage confidently, and told my best joke ever.

It was so funny. The only problem is... no one laughed.

I tried another one.

Luckily, one man laughed like crazy.

And it was... me.

My boss, eyes wide open, like he was trying to say, "*Wow, we'll call you next time, when we need to silence the audience.*"

I didn't know that I have such a weird "superpower": Tell a joke and shut people up.

So, I went to ask my mentor, Mr. Google. "*How to get rid of that superpower?*"

Then I found a video of Darren Lacroix, the Toastmasters world champion in 2001.

It was so amazing!

In 8 minutes, he made the audience laugh 23 times, and he inspired me to set a goal: Make people in my company laugh.

Have you ever tried something impossible?

I have...

In 9 minutes, I made everyone in my company laugh 24 times.

How?

First, I walked onto the stage, confidently...

Then, I played that video of Darren LaCroix.

Yeah, 23 laughs.

The last one was simple.

I just said to them, "Soon, I'll become a great speaker like him!"

That's 24.

Everybody, including my boss, laughed at my dream, louder than ever... (Maybe too loud)

The brick of reality hit my soul.

You know, the higher the hope, the bigger the despair. I thought to myself, “Maybe, I’ll never become a speaker. My dream is just a joke. This path is probably only for people who are already good at speaking. For someone introverted like me, it's just a crazy dream...”

One year later...

"Congratulations," my boss said, smiling. "You're now the company's official speaker."

I was stunned, speechless.

Looking back, I still can't believe that in 2012, I became the company's official speaker, just one year after setting that goal. Most people took years... and maybe gave up.

Not only that, in the company's training program, I was assigned to teach many theoretical parts. But then, the students' ratings at the end of the course still gave me 5 stars, both for the useful content and the lively, humorous presentation. I've dedicated over 1500 hours of training to my company, making tens of thousands of students laugh.

I'm sharing these achievements not to brag, because it's nothing compared to many people out there. I'm sharing it to show you the difference between me then and now.

At the end of 2015, I started my journey as a freelance writer, traveling and writing, and... having babies (I mean, light-weight thing, but heavy with knowledge, which are the books). Many readers have shared that they find my books not only valuable in terms of knowledge, but also easy to understand and humorous.

I used to be afraid of being in front of the camera, but at the end of 2021, I started the Tiktok channel @fususu.official. Thanks to the same humorous presentation techniques, within a few months, the channel has reached nearly 300,000 followers with dozens of million-view clips, which surprised me.

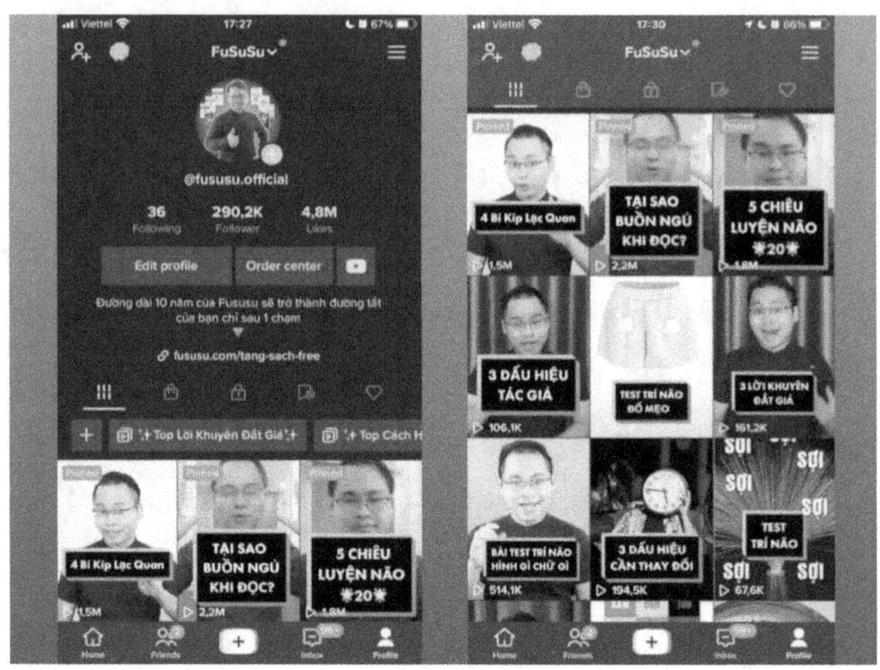

Then in May 2022, just one year after joining Toastmasters, I won first place in the District 97 Humorous Speech Contest. Because of Covid, the contest was held online, and I still remember the moment when the judges announced my name, I screamed like crazy in my room. Luckily, Zoom has a Mute button, otherwise I would have won another championship, for... the loudest contestant.

In 2023, my second year in Toastmasters, I received an even better award. It was my wife, and she works in a bank. My parents were so proud.

In 2024, with the secrets you'll discover in this book, I won first place in the Toastmasters International Speech Contest in District 97, and was the only one to make it to the Quarterfinals.

Currently, I'm living happily with my wife, in an apartment with an ocean view, in complete control of my own time. My daily work is writing books, and when I have free time, I coach, helping other writers start their writing journey, or turning their "abandoned" manuscripts into published books!

Once again, I'm not sharing this to brag. On my list, there are still many goals to achieve, dozens of books to write, hundreds of authors to support, and a lot of laughter I want to see from my readers (if you've been smiling while reading this, that's great)...

I'm sharing this to tell you:

> Anything is possible, it's all about the method. Sometimes, a little humor, even when you fail, is a way to inspire yourself to move forward. And the bricks that life throws at you are simply to help you build some foundation for your dreams.

What happened?

Are you curious about what happened that helped me change dramatically, not only advancing quickly in my career, but also having a free lifestyle from an early age?

In Particular, what method helped me become funny (in a natural way), helping me create bursts of laughter from the stage to the pages of a book (so that knowledge can stay in people's stomach longer?)

That's why I wrote this book.

As the saying goes, "Laughter is the best medicine." I believe that the louder you laugh, the happier and more prosperous you will be. Indeed...

- ★ Who doesn't love funny and endearing people?
- ★ Who doesn't cherish moments filled with laughter?
- ★ In a meeting with laughter, the stress bomb will explode into brilliant ideas.
- ★ In a difficult situation, humor can lift everyone's spirits.
- ★ A humorous remark can grab attention and make the listener focus more.
- ★ A humorous idea can attract customers and double sales.
- ★ Laughter is the fastest way to connect people.

And there are countless other benefits...

So, no matter what your starting point is, if you know how to tap into the treasure trove of laughter everywhere, your life will not only be more enjoyable, but your career will also take off like a kite in a gale.

Oh no, like a kite in a hurricane!

How will this book help you?

It's like a treasure chest filled with secrets that will make you naturally funny, both in your everyday life and on stage. These secrets aren't just things I learned from the world champions of public speakers, but also from over 10 years of using them myself!

But be careful... because if you learn these secrets well, you might become so funny that everyone in town will want you to be the host of every event! People will think of you when they think of fun and laughter!

The best part is that you can use these secrets in your conversations, on stage, and even in your writing. You can make people laugh, cry, or even both! A good book can make someone laugh or cry, but I think a really great book can do both!

An important note

Imagine each chapter of this book as a fun chat between us, sitting on a beautiful white sandy beach, sipping on a cool coconut drink, listening to the waves crashing gently...

So you can read any part of the book you want, or just read it from beginning to end. The most important thing is to use what you learn in real life, no matter what!

To help you understand better, I've also included some funny real-life situations that I created (or experienced), as well as quotes from my other books, or from some authors I've coached.

So what are you waiting for?

Turn the page to discover a big mistake that most people make when they try to be funnier, which often leads to some pretty bad consequences...

KEY #1
DON'T TELL JOKES

That's so weird, you want to make people laugh, so you tell a joke, right?

But you know that feeling when you tell a joke, and the only person laughing is you?

It's like a comedy show where you're both the actor and the audience. After acting out a funny scene, you run down to the audience and laugh, then run back up to the stage to keep acting...

It sounds really painful, doesn't it?

Your heart would even break if the audience was a whole crowd of people!

Is humor good for your heart?

I still remember that night, I stayed up all night looking for a few jokes. I was going to use them to start my presentation the next day, so I practiced a lot. When I got on stage, I told them with so much passion. It was amazing, everyone was laughing their heads off, I had a dream presentation!

Sorry, I was dreaming just now.

You know the truth. The first time I was trying to tell a joke on stage, I failed miserably. My heart was pounding, my hands were shaking, and I was sweating like I was taking a bath. I was so embarrassed, all my plans for the rest of the speech just crumbled like dominoes.

After that scary experience, I lost all faith in myself. Maybe an introvert like me, who's afraid of talking to people, the only way to make people laugh is to keep telling them about my crazy dream: Becoming a humorous public speaker.

Maybe humor isn't good for your heart like I thought. I don't want to have a heart attack like that again... But something inside me wouldn't let me give up. After that disastrous failure, I worked hard reading books, watching courses, researching how to tell jokes, and I realized that I had made a big mistake:

Telling jokes I found online.

Jokes can make one person laugh, but they also can confuse the other. It can even be a disaster if they've already heard it and know what you're going to say next. If they laugh, it's just a "pity laugh," meaning they feel that you’re so pitiful that they laugh for you.

So if you don't tell jokes, how do you make other people laugh?

Scan the QR code below, you'll see a live presentation of mine on the Toastmasters stage. Watch how I made the whole room laugh without telling a single joke!

leorowan.com/qrhumor1

What did I do?

Yeah, I didn't tell a joke, I told a real story.

Instead of telling jokes I found online or funny sayings that might not make people laugh, I told a real story that happened to me. So why did everyone laugh?

It's because of the interesting way I told it.

For example, in the video above, as soon as I got on stage, I asked the audience:

"Talking about confidence, have you ever given a presentation?"

(The audience nodded)

"Are you confident enough to... watch your recording?"

(The audience burst into laughter)

People laughed partly because I spoke their minds (everyone has been there), and mostly because of my "interesting perspective" on watching my own video: When you watch it, you need to have a lot of courage too! (A very educational horror movie)

Near the end of the video, you'll see me also reveal how I used to boost my confidence so I could "dare" to watch hundreds of my own video speech recordings. I bought popcorn and pretended I was watching a movie in a theater (at that time, the whole audience was either wide-eyed or laughing).

Or in my speech that won the Humorous Speech Toastmasters District 97 championship in 2022, in the opening part, after telling the audience about my failures (which I call "getting hit by bricks"), I ended with a line that made many people laugh and many people nod in agreement:

"The purpose of bricks is to build, not to destroy. If you're still alive after getting hit by bricks from everyone, pick up those bricks and build your dreams!"

They laughed because of the funny idea: If someone throws bricks at you, if you survive, dodge them and pick them up to... build a house, build your house of success (even build a skyscraper).

If you pay attention to the funny parts in my videos, or in the videos of world champion speakers, you'll see that they're all real stories, which were told with a humorous perspective in the present moment.

This is also how I used to make a lot of my students laugh back in the day, at my old training company, when talking about accelerated learning. Even though many years have passed, many students still remember the stories I told.

One of them is the story "My Secret Cheating Tool In Exams".

First, to understand why the students were rolling with laughter while I was telling the story, you need to know a little bit about the context at that time. Back then, I was a Trainer specializing in sharing accelerated learning methods, sharing 3 steps to create a creative mind map in each person's style.

Before that, I had projected a picture of the Mona Lisa on the slide, because it has a very special effect. It's that no matter where you are in the room, as long as you're looking at the slide, you always feel like Mona Lisa's eyes are looking at you. You can try to Google Mona Lisa's image, put it somewhere and move around the room to see if she's "watching" you!

And here's that presentation that I used to start off my sharing of learning methods.

"You know," I said to the students. "Back in college, there was this really hard subject called Philosophy. Getting a low score on the exam was normal. So what do you think we did about a month before the exam?"

One student shouted, "Study!"

"Excellent, you're a good student," I said. "Back then, we told each other: we have to... take advantage and have fun first! Because how can we play when the exam is near?"

(The students chuckled)

"So what did we do two weeks before the exam?" I asked the students.

The students said, "Study!"

"Great," I said. "We kept playing, even more enthusiastically..."

(The students laughed louder)

"So," I said. "One week before the exam, what did we do?"

The students all said in unison, "Play!"

I laughed. "You guys get me, but actually, one week before the exam, many of my friends went... to buy cheating tools!"

(The students roared with laughter)

"And you know, I was the class president, I had to be a good example. I couldn't buy cheat sheets, so what did I do?"

The students said, "Study?"

I replied, "I made my own cheat sheets."

(The students laughed their heads off)

"But don't get me wrong," I said, and showed a slide with a picture of a creative note I had made back then, looking like a code. "This is a special kind of cheat sheet, completely legal. Because after you create it, it will be imprinted in your brain, so you won't need to bring it into the exam room, but you can pull out knowledge from the whole chapter in your head!"

The students looked in awe at my special "homemade cheat sheet". I continued. "But it doesn't just pull out knowledge from my head, it also... pulls the invigilator!"

The students laughed again, many scratching their heads curiously. "Tell us!"

"Oh, that day in the exam room," I said. "My friends had prepared very carefully, with all kinds of different cheat sheets. But the thing is, no one dared to use them, because the invigilator... was very serious. He didn't move around, he just sat in one place and looked at everyone with eyes like... Mona Lisa."

(The whole room roared with laughter).

"Then," I continued, "I took a blank sheet of paper and drew all the code on it, then I started to look it up, decode it, and write it on my exam paper carefully. After a while, I suddenly felt a shadow on my exam paper..."

(The whole room held their breath)

I continued. "I looked up... and I jumped because I saw the Mona Lisa invigilator standing there, I don't know how long he had been there, and he was glaring at my code. And you know what my friends did at that time, when the invigilator was completely captivated by me?"

(The whole room shook their heads).

"What else could they do," I smiled. "They started to cheat. Whoever had a book used a book, whoever had a cheat sheet used a cheat sheet!"

(The whole room laughed)

"At the end of that exam, I got 8 out of 10 points in Philosophy," I clenched my hands together in a victorious pose. "Overall, my super cheat sheet not only saved my life, but also saved my teammates!"

(The whole room burst into laughter)

I said with enthusiasm. "And today, you will get to know the 3 secret steps to make... a super cheat sheet!"

(The whole room clapped wildly, some even stood on chairs, spinning their jackets, excited like their national football team was about to win the championship)

You see, it's a simple story that I could have told in a nutshell:

Back then, when I took the exam, I came up with a creative way to take notes that helped me pass the difficult exam, and today I'm going to share it with you students.

But if I had done that, I probably would have put the whole audience to sleep with theoretical steps, and I wouldn't have been chosen to be part of the company's dynamic and humorous Trainer team.

Instead, I brought the story to life, with humorous perspectives when I retold it, both creating laughter and generating excitement from the students as they received and applied the knowledge I was about to share.

And remember, in a post-course gathering, one student beamed and bragged to me, "Hey, thanks to your super cheat sheet, I got the first highest score in my life!"

In conclusion, the key secret to helping you be naturally funny is: Instead of trying to "add humor" with common jokes or collected funny stories, act like an archaeologist. "Unearth humor" by finding different and interesting perspectives on events that have happened to you, that many people might think are difficult, negative, or painful...

5 Benefits of Telling True Stories

When you know how to create laughter from your own true stories like that, you'll get a lot of benefits.

1) You avoid the risk of telling collected jokes or common jokes that everyone might already know.

First impressions are very important, if you go on stage and say things that everyone knows, then it will usually be very difficult to keep their attention afterwards.

2) Your personal story is always the most unique and different, it's the "VIP" card that helps your speech go straight to the audience's hearts.

Moreover, you will be more confident when telling your story, because... it's your story, you know it better than everyone, only you can tell it in detail.

3) At this point, whether people laugh or not doesn't matter. What matters is that you

achieve your goal: sharing your new perspective.

You will escape the burden of "having to be funny" and be more comfortable. The more comfortable you are, the more interesting your perspective, the louder they laugh, it's just a consequence.

4) True stories help you increase connection, and it's also easier to learn the lesson and apply it in the real world.

No one wants to be a "lab rat", they want some applications that work in real life, not in your fictional stories.

5) Not only can you present it on stage or in books, you can apply it to many different areas of your life.

Wherever there is communication, where there is human connection, there is an opportunity for you to tell stories. The truth is that many deals, many collaborations are closed thanks to stories.

Some examples in writing

Example #1

This example comes from a student in my book writing course. In the introduction, she tells the story of how she had to go to the hospital and met the coldest nurse in the world, who made her go to the pharmacy to buy saline solution for an IV. She wrote:

I couldn't believe my ears. How could she treat someone who's about to die like that? What if something happened to me on my way out?

Even though I was completely disappointed, I didn't want to go to heaven and be asked why I was there, and then have to answer: because I argued with a nurse.

So, *I had to turn around and go back to the pharmacy. The 30-meter walk felt like a mile...*

You see, the humor doesn't come from the nurse making her go buy saline solution, but from the way she reacted and shared her thoughts at the time, and her thoughts when she recounted it.

Example #2

Another student of mine, even though the content of his book is about divorce and how to recover happiness, also has many stories told with a humorous perspective that made me laugh. Among them, I was most impressed by a story he told about a time when he and his wife had a loud argument. He wrote:

Because she was so angry, my wife immediately threw my phone at the wall. At that moment, my hands and feet were itching terribly, and my head felt like it was about to explode. I couldn't control my emotions, and immediately grabbed my wife's iPhone and threw it hard on the floor.

After that, I realized that in terms of emotions, my wife might be stronger, but when it comes to arm strength and throwing power, I was superior. My wife's phone wouldn't turn on, and I had to be the one to take it to get repaired.

You see, even when recounting a not-so-pleasant event, he even analyzes the connection between emotions and throwing power. It's that unexpected twist that makes it funny!

Example #3

This example is from another student, she turned many simple stories in life into humor by changing her perspective. She wrote:

Bang!

I crashed into the transparent glass door with a searing pain. Earlier, there were too many mosquitoes in the house, and I closed the door without realizing it. Speaking of mosquitoes, I'm so angry. I don't need to spend money to get a bunch of tattoos on my calves.

Suddenly... The pain in my head was like an electric shock. I realized, "Instead of feeding these guys, my blood should have a greater meaning, right?"

So I *decided: I must donate blood to a hospital.*

You see, a story that could be simply told as "I got bitten by mosquitoes, so... I donated blood" becomes so lively under her storytelling.

I bet you can guess what the common feature of these 3 stories is?

It's the same event, but when you recount it with different thoughts, people's brains are naturally stimulated, and laughter is easily created naturally.

This is also the secret of the champions of public speaking. This secret has made their speeches not only naturally humorous, but also helped them deliver their message to the audience more easily and deeply.

You can scan the QR code below to watch the 2013 World Champion of Public Speaking by

Presiyan Vasilev, where he recounts a simple experience with a tire, but how it changed his life.

leorowan.com/qrhumor2

You should watch before you read on. If you've watched the clip and paid attention, you'll see that the story is really simple, right?

That day, my tire went flat, someone helped me lift it, and I realized: don't be afraid to ask for help.

If that's the case, then Presiyan probably wouldn't have won the world champion of public speaking, and he would have won some kind of tire-lifting expert contest.

Practice changing your perspective

Let's see if you can find a positive angle for these common events. Then you can compare your ideas with mine below. The more you read and practice, the better you'll understand and become more skilled.

1) Many people are very afraid of failure...

When it comes to failure, everyone is afraid. So, what interesting perspective can you have on failure?

Leo: Failure is like a stumble. Stumbling, sometimes, is a faster way to move forward (and later, your book might be thicker).

2) No one likes criticism...

Especially bad mouthing behind your back. What interesting perspective can you have?

Leo: When someone talks bad behind your back, it means they're... behind you. Thanks to them being behind, you can easily move forward without any traffic jam! (Or you can consider them as "rear view mirrors", helping you see the things you need to improve).

3) How do you feel when you lose your job?

What interesting perspective can you have on this unwanted situation?

Leo: Sometimes, losing your job is the best time to... start your own business. Because then, you have nothing left to lose. And who knows, maybe that will be the last time you lose your job, and become a CEO?

4) No one likes sad memories...

But if they have a positive meaning, what could it be?

Leo: If everyone was born happy, it would be boring. Every pain is an asset, and who knows, it could become a great chapter of a novel, or even a movie later?

5) Have you ever been heartbroken?

Every time you recall it, it feels like your heart is breaking, right? How can we make it humorous?

Leo: Like many people, I've been heartbroken. Every time I think about it, my heart aches, but I still have to laugh, because I don't want to die of a heart attack...

6) Do you have a disease?

It's so annoying, you're fine and then you get sick, and you have to go to the hospital....

Leo: It could be a free "trip" to the hospital, who knows, you might meet a "handsome doctor, beautiful goddess"? This could also be a "secret blessing" from the universe, helping you "level up" your adaptability, "upgrade" your immune system, what do you think?

7) Stuck in a traffic jam

A very common situation, right? If you don't want to get angry, what will you think?

Leo: This could be a "golden opportunity" for you to "unearth" your hidden talents, like: singing opera, composing music, or writing movie scripts. Who knows, you might find breakthrough ideas to become a "star" on the "stage" of traffic jams!

The Difference To Stand-Up Comedy

Have you ever watched stand-up comedy shows?

This is a type of comedy where a performer usually talks directly to the audience. They can tell jokes, tell funny stories, even do magic tricks, sing, and so on... to entertain and relax the audience. I have also watched many stand-up comedy clips and laughed until I cried. However, with the same result of making people laugh, there is a big difference between a champion speaker and a stand-up comedian.

Watching a stand-up comedy show, people can laugh non-stop for an hour, but then they often don't remember any specific message. Because the purpose of stand-up comedians is to make the audience laugh, and the purpose of the audience is to be entertained.

With champion speakers, their most important goal is to convey a message. Laughter is just a tool to make that message more impressive. Whether the audience laughs or not, doesn't matter to them, as long as the message has been delivered.

In short, with stand-up comedy, laughter is the goal, while with humorous presentations, laughter is the means.

You can also understand it simply: one side is laughing to forget, the other is laughing to remember.

Stand-up comedy helps you laugh to forget your troubles, and also forget why you're laughing. Champions of public speaking make you laugh to remember the messages, remember the lessons to apply, and change.

So how do you create naturally funny speeches that make your audience excited and remember the message forever?

Let's turn the page to discover the most important secret I learned from the best world champions of public speaking.

KEY #2
HUMOR MINING

Craig Valentine—my teacher, also the 1999 world champion of public speaking—once said something I really like:

“Don’t add humor, uncover it!”

Have you ever been through something that you find funny now when you think back on it?

If you scan the QR code below, you'll see my speech about the first time I got bitten by a dog, which brought a lot of laughter at the 2024 Toastmasters International Speech Contest at District 97 and got me the first prize. You should watch it before reading on, because I'll be analyzing a lot of details in it.

leorowan.com/qrhumor3

You see, the truth is that laughter is already there, somewhere in your experiences. But at that time, you might be too busy "playing the main character" with mixed emotions, so you couldn't laugh.

Now, thinking back on that memory and telling it is what makes it funny. Imagine if I had rolled around laughing after being bitten by a dog, where would they take me? ●

Where is the gold mine of humor?

You might think humor often comes from unexpected situations in life, like:

1) *Someone trying to do something but failing.*

I once saw a clip on Facebook, a father who saw his child slip and fall on the floor. He immediately rushed to help the child, but also slipped and bumped into the child, causing it to slide like flying across the floor. The clip was shared a lot, with laughing emojis.

2) *Someone encountering a ridiculous situation because of their own clumsiness.*

Someone trying to park a car in a very tight spot, after a lot of struggle they finally did it, and felt like a superhero. Then, they realized that because the spot was too tight, they couldn't open the car door. To get out, they had to back up the car and finally had to find another parking spot.

3) A situation that no one would think could happen.

A true story from a friend of mine:

That night, coming home from work, when she went to the parking lot, she struggled to open the motorbike lock. She called her coworker for the motorcycle rescue number, then went back to the office to wait for it to cool down.

Later, when the mechanic arrived, the security guard wouldn't let him in, so she had to take the motorbike out to get it fixed. When the mechanic was about to break the lock, she realized that she had put the wrong key in the motorbike next to hers.

The two motorbikes were the same type, parked next to each other, only the license plate was different. Luckily, she realized it before breaking the other person's motorbike!

And there are many other unexpected situations that often bring laughter in life. However, if that's all there is, then the champions of humorous presentations, or stand-up comedians, would spend their days praying:

"Please give me an unexpected situation today, the more ridiculous the better!"

Actually, a place that helps you easily dig up humor, without having to put yourself in awkward situations, is the dialogue, the thoughts of the characters, and even the thoughts (possibly) of the audience, which will also become a gold mine of laughter.

For example, if you watch the clip in the QR code at the beginning of this chapter, I have dug up humor many times from my own thoughts, or from the characters in the story:

A tiny spider bit Peter on the neck, making him Spiderman. I was bitten on the butt by a big black dog, how would I transform?

On the red Honda, my dad took me to the scariest place on earth: the pet store.

My little dog charged at the ferocious dog, like a sidekick in a movie, sacrificing himself to save the hero (me).

Reading face, guessing mind

One of the places where you can find the most laughter is in the dialogue of characters in stories. So, if you feel like your story is boring, it might be because you're telling it like a news report and you're missing out on the cool things the characters say, or the interesting things they might be thinking.

What's a news report style of storytelling?

It's simple, you focus on the main events:

That day, a dog bit me. Since then, I've been really scared of dogs. My dad bought me a small dog to help me get over my fear.

The end!

What's a lively way to tell a story?

It's when you breathe life to the story, like I did in my speech, so people feel like they're watching a movie and they realize something interesting. Don't worry, when you tell a story in a real way, it doesn't mean you have to tell every boring detail that happened.

You're the director of the story, you can put your own new (and funny) thoughts from right now into those boring situations that happened before.

This is a special trick I like to use to show what my characters might be thinking and make my stories more exciting.

I call it: "Reading Face, Guessing Mind."

Do you remember these details from my first story about the dog bite?

"The little dog looked at me like he wanted to say: My hero, the best way to overcome your fear is to have fun with me..."

In the story I told you at the beginning of this book, I also uncovered some humor when I told my parents about my dream of becoming a great speaker. Do you remember that?

Dad's face turned red, "Are you crazy?"

(Later, the one who actually went crazy was... him)

Mom just smiled, looking at me, as if to say, "A great speaker? Does it have bluetooth?"

The brick of doubt hit my heart.

You see, it's all just thoughts, a new way of looking at things, all in my imagination. It's based on a real moment when my mom was kinda doubtful about my dream. And everyone laughs because of how I tell the story, and because of how I imagine things, not because of the actual story itself (which was actually pretty sad and boring).

Again, where do you think they'd take me after I got yelled at but still laughed my head off?

Remember: You don't need to make anyone laugh, you just need to share a different and interesting point of view. When you can be happy with your own story, then everyone's laughter is just a consequence.

You could even add your current thoughts about yourself back then.

For example, if I were telling the dog bite story in a different presentation about teamwork, after the part where I got bitten, I could say:

"If I knew about the power of teamwork back then, I probably would have called my friends the next day to deal with that dog. My fear would have disappeared right away..."

If you read a lot of my books, you'll see this story about me getting bitten by a dog pop up again and again, but with different messages. I don't have to go looking for a new dog every time I give a new talk or write a new book.

When you use this trick, you can uncover humor many times over one single story. This trick will save you a lot of energy, right?

My book writing students often use these "humor mining" techniques in their books. Remember the author with the muscular hands who "transformed" his wife's phone in tip #1? See how he uncovered humor in the story of him getting his wife's phone fixed:

I still remember the look on the phone repair guy's face that day. He said, "Wow, what happened to this phone?"

"I gave it a new life!" I explained.

His face went from confused to terrified, his eyes darting between me and the phone, like it was the sickest "patient" he'd ever seen, with the cause still a mystery.

At that moment, I remembered the random, impulsive thing I did a few days before and found it hilarious. The more physical force you use, the more it affects your heart afterward.

My heart sank when I imagined having to pay a lot of money to fix that phone.

Luckily, I didn't have to fix it. The repair guy said the "phone patient" had a terminal illness and couldn't be saved.

You see, instead of just saying "I took the phone to get fixed, and the guy shook his head and said it was completely broken," he showed us a little movie in our minds.

To help you use this trick, I've put together 6 golden phrases to help you dig up the treasure of humor in situations that have already happened, and tell them in a funny and natural way.

6 Golden Phrases to Mine Humor

1) [Someone] looked at me with eyes (or a face) like they wanted to say, "[something surprising]."

2) What would happen (or what do you think) if... [an interesting hypothetical situation]

3) You might think... [an interesting thought that your readers/audience might have]

4) Looking back, I see... [a funny perspective]

5) If I had known back then... [about something], I would have... [a funny idea]

6) That feeling was like... [an interesting, relatable comparison]

3 Steps to Mine Humor

So, you've learned a big secret of champion speakers, a secret that makes their talks naturally funny:

Humor can come from unexpected situations in life, but if you rely on "luck" for it, your results will be pretty random too. That's why the champions focus on interesting perspectives when they tell their stories.

And the secret to mining humor from any story can be summed up in 3 steps:

Step 1) Write in Detail using S.H.E.

Write your story in as much detail as possible, making sure it has all the S.H.E. elements: See, Hear, Experience.

- What did you See?
- What did you Hear?
- What emotions did you Experience?

Like a map, the more detail you write, the more opportunities you'll find to mine laughter in every detail.

Step 2) Apply the 6 Golden Phrases

Just thinking about it, or reading your story once, might not give you ideas right away, but it'll be different if you read it over and over again.

The authors I train directly, we often go over and over our books, writing them at least 10 times, some even 15 or 20 times. That's how you can "mine" those valuable details that you might have missed before.

Read your story over and over again, and try applying each phrase to each part of your story and see what happens.

Step 3) Try Telling it, Share it with Someone

If you tell it and they laugh, great! You've struck a vein of humor gold. If they don't laugh, that's okay, you're still safe, because your main goal isn't to make them laugh, it's to share your interesting perspective, and laughter is just a result.

The important thing is to learn from it for the next time, so your story gets better and funnier.

Where to Tell Your Stories?

It would be risky to bring your untold stories to a big stage, especially if people have paid to hear you speak, right?

So, you need a safe environment to practice. You can join stand-up comedy clubs, but personally, I like to join Toastmasters. It's a positive environment where you can get feedback to help you improve quickly.

Especially because it's international, you can join anywhere, and there are events and competitions on a global scale every year for you to test yourself. I've even founded a few Toastmasters clubs like ACI Online Toastmasters and C-Level Advanced Toastmasters. The clubs I've founded usually operate online, so you can join us too.

fb.com/aci.toastmasters.official

c-level.toastmastersvn.com

Or, if you're not afraid, you can try writing the story again and posting it on your personal Facebook, see if anyone laughs. Even safer and faster is to join the Anyone Can Write Facebook group at the end of the book, where everyone practices their writing skills.

By now, you've learned about the biggest mistake in humor, and you've also learned the biggest principle of natural humor. The next part is a principle hidden behind many jokes or funny speeches.

KEY #3

SET—UP—PUNCH

Have you ever read a joke and wondered why you laughed?

Especially, how do they make you laugh?

Here's a classic 3-step formula (that few know), used in jokes. Stand-up comedians from amateurs to professionals use them to create laughter like an explosion on stage.

What is set—up—punch?

Read the stories below, see if you can guess.

Story #1: Three Wishes

There were three best friends stranded on a deserted island. After many days, they found a magic lamp, a genie appeared and said he would grant them three wishes.

The first guy said, "I wish I could go home right now!"

The genie snapped his fingers, he disappeared.

The second guy was so happy, he said, "I wish that too!"

The genie snapped his fingers, he disappeared.

The third guy, with a sad face, said. "It's so lonely here, I wish my friends would come back."

Story #2: The Duck Who Likes Grapes

A duck walks into a store and asks, "Do you have any grapes?"

The shopkeeper says, "No, sorry, I don't have any grapes."

The next day, the duck comes back and asks: "Do you have any grapes?"

"No!" the shopkeeper said, with a frown. "If you come back tomorrow asking for grapes again, I'll nail your beak to the floor!"

The next day, the duck comes back and asks: "Do you have any nails?"

The shopkeeper says, "No."

The duck asks, "Do you have any grapes?"

I told these two stories to my students in my book writing class. They laughed their heads off.

So what exactly is a "set-up-punch"? Have you figured it out yet?

It's a formula for surprise, based on a principle of how our brains work. Our brains automatically guess and fill in the blanks with the information we're given.

In the story of the three wishes, the first guy wishes to go home. Our brains think that's normal (set). Then, the second guy also wishes to go home, and our brains are even more convinced that's normal (up).

The third guy, because of the set-up, our brains tend to think he'll also wish to go home. When he says that wish, our brains are surprised (punch) and we laugh. Or, our brains might think he'll wish for something different, but they don't expect him to make such a silly wish (strong punch).

Similarly, in the story of the duck who loves grapes, the first time the duck asks if there are any grapes, our brains are set up (set). The second time he asks, and the owner yells at him, most people will think the third time he'll ask something different (up). The third time, he does ask something different (our brains aren't surprised), but then he cleverly goes back to the original question to achieve his goal. This makes our brains really surprised (strong punch) and we laugh.

The Essence of Set—Up—Punch

To use the Set—Up—Punch successfully, you need to understand how it works:

Set: You give information A in direction X.

Up: You continue to give information B in direction X, so that the brain believes the next information will also be in direction X.

Punch: You give information D, in direction Y, which is opposite to X.

Let's look at another example to see if you can identify which part is Set, which is Up, and which is Punch?

What are you most proud of? I used to set a goal to become a speaker, and now, I have over 2,000 hours of speaking experience...

I used to set a goal to become an author, and by now, I've published over 10 books...

I used to set a goal to lose weight, and right now, I'm still the same...

Note: The funny effect will be less strong if you use this formula too many times at once, or if you tell it too slowly, giving the listener's brain time to guess what will happen.

So, if you use it, you need to set it up cleverly, so that people's brains have a hard time guessing what the punchline will be.

Also, you need to practice beforehand, so you can tell it smoothly, with a serious face... the more serious, the better, usually. That's when it's most effective.

Practice Set-Up-Punch

Actually, this formula is very common, especially in jokes and stand-up comedy shows. And the most effective way to practice this formula is through "imitation".

Many people often read jokes or watch comedy shows only once for entertainment. If you want to improve your sense of humor, watch them again and again, and ask yourself:

- Set: Where was I "set up" the first time?
- Up: How was I "set up" the second time?
- Punch: Where was I "punched"? (usually the line that made you laugh).

Now, let's practice!

Spotting the Set-Up-Punch

Here are a few of my favorite jokes. Enjoy them the first time, then read them again and try to find the set-up and punchline elements.

1) The Ugly Child

A woman and her child boarded a bus. The driver said, "Goodness, that's the ugliest kid I've ever seen!"

She was furious. When she sat down in the back row, she told a man sitting next to her, "The driver just insulted me!"

The man looked very upset. "Go up there and give him a piece of your mind. And don't worry, I'll hold your monkey."

2) Mad Cow Disease

On a field, three cows were chatting.

The first cow said, "Have you guys heard about this mad cow disease spreading?"

"Yes," said the second cow, trembling. "It's supposed to be terrible. Thankfully, it hasn't reached here yet."

"That's right," said the third cow. "We're so lucky to be penguins."

3) Calling for Help

Two people were walking in the woods when one suddenly collapsed, his face turning pale. The other pulled out his phone and called 911.

"Hello, I think my friend has fainted," he yelled. "What should I do?"

The operator said, "Stay calm. First, make sure they're actually fainted..."

Then there was a moment of silence, followed by a loud smack. Back on the phone, he said. "Okay, now what?"

4) The Bean Jar

A newly married couple bought two jars and agreed that whenever either of them thought badly of the other, they would put a bean in the other person's jar.

When they got old, after eating their afternoon porridge, they watched the sunset together beside the two jars. The husband was very emotional.

He said, "Honey, I'm so sorry..."

He opened his jar, and there were about 30 beans inside.

It was the wife's turn. She opened her jar, and there were only a few beans inside.

The husband cried. The wife patted his shoulder and said, "It's okay, honey, I'm sorry too. We ran out of rice, so I used all the beans from my jar to make porridge."

5) Will We Escape?

Two people were walking in the woods when they encountered a leopard. Immediately, one of them took off his backpack, grabbed his running shoes, and put them on.

"What are you doing?" the other yelled. "We can't run faster than it, even with running shoes."

"Why does it matter?" the other replied. "I just need to run faster than you."

6) Doctor's Announcement

A doctor called his patient and said, "I have bad news and worse news. The bad news is you only have 24 hours to live."

"That's bad," the patient replied. "What could be worse?"

The doctor answered, "I've been trying to reach you since yesterday and you haven't answered your phone."

7) Dad's Confession

One evening, I went to visit my son. I asked him to borrow his newspaper. "Can I borrow your newspaper, son?"

"Dad, this is the 21st century," my son said. "I don't have a newspaper, but if you like, you can use my iPad."

I can tell you this: That spider never knew what hit it.

Well, did you have some fun?

Your brain is very smart. Once you understand the principle and see many examples, the Set-Up-Punch will seep into every cell of your brain, becoming a reflex. And one day, you will naturally come up with ideas for set-ups and punchlines in your writing, and even in your conversations.

Just like some people have the ability to "speak in poetry," you will develop the ability to "speak with laughter."

The Giant Elephant Story

Remember that time, during a Toastmasters Club meeting in Da Nang, I participated as the General Evaluator (the person who gives the report at the end of the meeting, and everyone usually calls G.E).

When it was my turn, I walked onto the stage and said, "What do you think G.E stands for?"

"General Evaluator..." everyone said in unison.

I nodded and said, "It's short for Giant Elephant."

The whole room burst into laughter. Then I explained why that "giant elephant" was related to the evaluation role. Everyone was very convinced and listened attentively from beginning to end.

Why did everyone laugh?

Set: Because when mentioning G.E, everyone usually thinks of General Evaluator, a very familiar role in Toastmasters meetings.

Up: Mentioning this keyword, everyone's brains were already set up, and then they all shouted "General Evaluator" in unison, so their brains were set up again.

Punch: That's why when I punched with a new and unusual answer, the whole room immediately erupted in laughter (it could also be because I looked as chubby as a giant elephant).

Not to mention, every time I mentioned the image of the elephant afterwards, everyone laughed. For example, later, when it was my turn to speak again, I greeted everyone with, "Hello, your Giant Elephant is here..."

And you might think, "Wow, that's amazing, how did Fususu come up with the idea that G.E is a Giant Elephant?"

I won't hide it from you, I asked ChatGPT beforehand, "What interesting things could G.E stand for?"

And Giant Elephant was one of the ideas that OpenAI came up with. It's amazing to have technology to help, isn't it?

But one thing to note is that if you ask AI to tell a joke, or make your story funnier... I think you'll be disappointed right now. Because AI's concept of humor seems different from ours.

So, you still need to understand the important principles, so that if you do ask AI for help, you'll know what you're looking for.

Quick Setup, Strong Punchline

In many speeches, sometimes this 3-step method can be simplified to 2 steps: Setup & Punchline, or more fully: "Quick Setup - Strong Punchline."

The easiest example is in my speech on the Toastmasters stage about confidence. Do you remember how I started my speech?

"Speaking of confidence, I have two questions for you:

1) *Have you ever given a presentation? (setup)*

2) *Are you confident when you watch your video recording? (punchline)"*

Right after that, the audience burst into laughter.

In the set-up, I talked about confidence, which is a pretty "serious" topic. People's brains assumed that what I said next would be similar, or some kind of speaking secret. Then, with the second question, they were surprised when I mentioned something related to themselves.

To use this technique effectively, you need to understand the audience's psychology very well, so you can speak to their hidden thoughts and pain.

For example, I still remember in a speech by Darren Lacroix, the 2001 speech champion, he walked onto the stage and said:

"Have you ever given a speech, where you look very confident on the outside (setup), but on the inside, you're doing aerobics? (punchline)"

Of course, when he said that, Darren also used his body language very effectively. When he got to the aerobics part, he simultaneously held a water bottle and shook it so it splashed all over the floor, making the comedic effect even stronger.

You could say that Toastmasters speech champions are all experts in "Quick Setup & Strong Punchline."

The good news is that since 2012, most of the champion speeches have been uploaded by Toastmasters. You can google the keyword "Toastmasters speech champion" to watch these interesting speeches, so your brain can absorb the principle of Setup & Punchline.

You can also scan the QR code below to watch Darren Lacroix's clip.

leorowan.com/clip-champion-1

If you feel that Setup & Punchline is a bit hard to apply because you haven't come up with an idea yet, don't worry too much. It takes practice for your brain to get used to "bending" other people's mind.

Furthermore, the next secrets are very easy to apply, and also based on this principle of Setup & Punchline, with many specific examples. Keep exploring to understand more and see their applications in real life!

KEY #4
MIND BENDING

I'm a shy person. Talking to people is hard, making them laugh is even harder. But I found a special strength that introverts have, that can help them be funny.

Unexpected Responses

Back in 2019, I was alone in Quy Nhon, Vietnam. To feel less lonely, I joined an English class. We had a new teacher named Jack, from a small island near Florida, USA.

He started the class by asking everyone to list things you might find in a kitchen.

"A knife," said a girl.

"A cabinet," said a boy.

"My mom," I said.

The whole class laughed. I scored my first point on my journey to being funny.

"Anything else?" Jack asked.

I continued. "Maybe... a cat?"

The class laughed again.

At the end of class, Jack said, "Everyone could ask me anything, except *How old am I*?"

I asked right away, "How young are you?"

This time, Jack laughed.

You see, I don't talk much (because I'm shy), but every time I do, the whole class laughs.

The strength I'm talking about is the ability to observe and listen. Especially the ability to know what people are thinking.

There were many other times in that English class where I made the whole class laugh. The one I remember best was when we welcomed a new French teacher named Sonar. One day, he had us talk about family trees. He drew a diagram on the board, showing the relationships between family members.

"Above you are your parents," Mr. Sonar asked. "So what's above your parents?"

"Grandparents," a classmate answered.

"So what's above your grandparents?"

I raised my hand and said, "Adam and Eve?"

The whole class laughed.

Next, Mr. Sonar asked. "Okay, we have cousins, aunt, uncle. So someone who marries your uncle would be..."

I raised my hand and confidently said, "My uncle's wife?"

The class laughed again.

That day was great, because we got to drink a lot of good medicine, the kind that makes you laugh. You see, there's a really easy place to uncover humor: in conversations.

Sometimes, you don't need to say much. Just be bold and share your different opinion when asked. This is called mind bending.

What is "mind-bending"?

Can you guess why most people laugh at my "foolish" answers above?

It's because my "naive" answers surprised everyone.

When Jack asked everyone to list the things in the kitchen, he used the phrase "things in the kitchen," so when everyone chose objects (things that are able to move), I chose things that are moveable.

Then Sonar drew a family tree and gave a bunch of proper nouns like cousins, aunt to refer to people who are related to you. Then Sonar asked what you would call your uncle's spouse, most people would think it would be some kind of complex proper noun, so they laughed when I gave the simplest answer:

"My uncle's wife."

And when Sonar asked what's above grandparents, most people might think about their grandparents or something like that, but they wouldn't go as far as the "source" of the family tree like me:

Adam and Eve.

When they were surprised like that, they laughed. This is also the principle of mind-bending. Simply, you figure out what most people are thinking and come up with a different idea, the more naive it is like a child, the better.

That's in real-life conversations, but what about presentations, writing, or when you need to present an idea?

The good news is that you can totally apply this mind-bending technique.

Mind-bending in presentations

Have you ever heard this saying?

“If you want to go fast, go alone, if you want to go far, go together.”

But what happens if you go with... a bunch of fools?

Did you just laugh?

If you did, this principle has worked.

This is a simple application of mind-bending in presentations, which is essentially a "set-up & punch" method that involves two steps:

1) You give out information X, something that as many people know, or the easier it is to agree, the better.

2) You give out information X' to bend their mind, making them surprised. The more different the idea, the easier it is to make people laugh.

To help you understand more about mind-bending, let's look at some examples. The more you see, the more your brain will learn, imitate, and you will understand and apply it more easily.

So, I've prepared for you...

20 mind-bending examples

A note, these examples are just examples, they may "challenge" some positive beliefs, but they are not a substitute for life advice.

1) *"Nothing is impossible!"*

Have you ever tried to put toothpaste back in the tube after squeezing it out?

2) *"Knowledge is power."*

When you're walking in the park and suddenly a vicious dog charges at you, what knowledge will give you the power to fight it?

3) *"Diligence makes up for lack of intelligence."*

But what if you diligently apply a wrong method?

4) *Some people say, "Life is like a game, you need to know the rules."*

I wonder, where is the "replay" button?

5) *Many people advise, "Live as if today is your last day."*

I think that's a great idea, but if so, who will hire me? Who will need someone to work one day and then disappear?

6) *"Never give up..."*

That's right, unless you're running a marathon and find out you're running in the opposite direction from everyone else!

So, sometimes knowing when to quit is a wise way to move forward.

7) *"Money can't buy happiness..."*

That's right, so give me all your money, I'll prove to you that money can make someone happy.

Money may not buy happiness, but it can make someone happy, and you'll be happy too!

8) *"Love is above all."*

That's right, but have you ever tried paying bills with love?

9) "The most important thing is not winning, but participating wholeheartedly..."

Right, but try telling that to someone who just lost a bet and lost a lot of money.

10) "Sometimes the smallest things make the biggest difference..."

Great, like the small stone you accidentally tripped over that made you fall and break your face.

11) "Time is money."

That's right, it's just a pity that sometimes I'm too free, but I can't convert that time into gold and silver.

12) "Stay away from negative people."

But what if that negative person is your boss?

13) "Always smile."

Okay, try smiling when you're having your teeth pulled. Your humor is sure to "level up"!

14) "*Age is just a number.*"

But sometimes that number will determine whether you get a discount on movie tickets.

15) "*Follow your dreams!*"

But what if your dream is to become a superhero?

16) "*Health is the most valuable asset.*"

What if you don't have money for medical treatment? Money also has its role.

17) "*Happiness is a journey, not a destination.*"

But what if that journey is too long and tiring? And there's no one funny to go with?

18) "*Forgive others.*"

Good. But what if they've hurt you so many times that it's "challenging" you?

19) "*Enjoy the present moment.*"

But what if something is on fire at the moment?

20) *"Everything happens for a reason."*

So what's the reason I just tripped and fell down the stairs?

You see the power of mind-bending, right?

Also, mind-bending when used in combination with set-up-punch is incredibly powerful. Do you remember the story about taking the exam using cheat sheets that I told you in the secret #1?

Actually, I applied the set-up-punch very flexibly with mind-bending, to constantly make the students laugh, especially at the beginning, when I asked the students to guess what we did before the exam.

If you've forgotten, you can flip back and read it again, or see my summary and analysis:

- First, I asked them what we would do a month before the exam?
- Most people would think it's studying.
- My answer was... to take advantage of playing. Everyone laughed because they were surprised.

- Then I asked again: What about 2 weeks before the exam?
- Most students would think it's just studying, but the answer was still playing.
- That led to when I asked what about 1 week before the exam?
- It could be studying, because the previous two times were wrong, so most students would think it's playing.
- I said "you understand me" to set-up the students' brains so that they might be right, but then I gave the unexpected answer... "buy cheat sheets".

By constantly taking everyone from one surprise to another that they couldn't predict, I created roaring laughter.

Practice in life

Mind-bending is not just a technique for making people laugh, but also a habit that helps you think differently all the time, everywhere.

I really like this way, because when you come up with a different way of thinking, whether people laugh or not, they still find it very interesting.

So, you can practice it in your daily life, with the following suggestions:

1) Social media posts

You can pay attention to social media posts, see what the poster is trying to convey. Then, you read to see what most people comment, then try to come up with a different thought. You can start with the following sentences:

- What if...
- I agree, but...
- Do you think...

Practice using these 3 sentences a lot, I call them the creative thinking stimulating sentences.

2) Common beliefs

You list what most people believe in, what are some popular sayings that are being shared widely.

Then, you try to dig deeper, find aspects that no one pays attention to, like in the mind-bending example above.

Once you've found an idea, you can totally post an article sharing that saying and your new thoughts.

3) Unexpected responses

Once you're used to mind-bending through writing, you can actively "respond" in real-life situations like I did in my English class (instead of "being stuck" when asked).

Simply listen, observe, and pay attention to how most people will think, or what kind of trend they will answer, and when it's your turn, answer in a different way.

Of course, you should try to "mind-bend" intelligently, related to the topic everyone is discussing. Avoid "bending" too much, even "breaking" everyone's calm nerves, then it's hard to predict your outcome.

More mind-bending examples

This technique can also be used in writing, especially in writing stories, novels.

Example in Numagician - The Magic Numbers and Untold Stories

This book brings together stories about the vibrant numbers in the kingdom of Numagician as told by the Six-Nine bird, which has brought a lot of laughter to young readers.

Here is an excerpt from the story about the Three-Seven monkey, to see if you can spot the mind-bending part:

Who do you think benefits the most from competitions? The athletes, because they will be famous? Or the audience, because they will get to see exciting matches? In my opinion, it's the organizers, because they are the ones selling tickets, and Three-Seven Monkey is the most talented organizer I've ever known...

I met the Three-Seven monkey once when I went to watch the monkey's banana-picking climbing competition. At that time, he was just a janitor, cleaning up the flattened bananas on the ground, the leftover product after each competition. A few years later, I met him again, he had become the head organizer, with an income of millions of Susu.

Example in Numagician - Awaken the Creative Artist Within

This is a collection of 100 super short stories, to help you remember what each number corresponds to, so there are a lot of funny stories. A typical example is the story of the Two-Seven harp.

This is the magical Two-Seven harp, it has exactly 27 strings with 27 different colors. Anyone who hears the music will be enchanted and follow the words sung by the singer (no matter how bad they sing).

Long ago, the mermaid sisters used the Two-Seven harp to lure handsome sailors to... wash dishes. But after discovering that the number of broken dishes was increasing, the mermaid sisters were fed up and left for another planet, leaving the Two-Seven guitar moldy at the bottom of the ocean.

A fisherman picked up the Two-Seven harp and used it to open classes on "resisting temptation." Graduates all possess a peaceful, strong mind, nothing can shake their will.

The Team & Building Story

That time we went on a Toastmasters Team Building trip to Da Lat, Vietnam. It was raining nonstop and freezing cold, so a lot of the activities didn't go as planned, and the person in charge had to make some pretty big changes.

When I saw them looking a little down, sharing with everyone how the plans kept changing, you know what I said?

I said, "It's Team Building. First you have a **team**, then you **build** the plan."

Everyone burst out laughing, and the whole room felt warmer. Everyone realized, "Yeah, having the team is good enough, getting to see each other is amazing..."

Another time, my wife, Giang Rita, and I went to a Toastmasters club in Da Nang, Vietnam. That day, I was assigned to be the evaluator for her speech. Before Giang spoke, I was invited to introduce the purpose of her speech, which was going to focus on Body Language.

I stood up confidently, but somehow my mouth stuttered and I said, "Today, we'll focus on her body... and language."

The whole room erupted in laughter.

Right after that, I tried to recover, "I mean, body language is also a language."

Team and Building, Body and Language...

Actually, this is also a new humor technique that's really easy to use. Let's explore it in the next chapter!

KEY #5
WORDPLAY

Have you ever read a story or a book and laughed your head off? Do you want to write in a humorous way like that author?

I have some bad news and some good news for you.

The bad news...

Writing funny stuff is actually much harder than talking or giving a funny speech.

Why is that?

It's simple:

> Listening is natural, reading is a skill.

Most people learn to listen from the time they are born, while reading takes a lot of hard work in school. Usually, not many people get good grades in Literature, which leads to a general reluctance to read.

Plus, the average reading speed of adults is about 200-300 words per minute, but the brain's sound processing speed can be up to 800 words per minute.

If you want to check this out, scan the QR code below, you'll see a clip of me talking at rocket speed, over 500 words per minute, and you can still understand the content! (Note. You might need to enable the auto-translated caption on your Tiktok App)

leorowan.com/qrhumor4

Isn't it amazing how fast your brain can process sounds?

That's both a strength and a weakness, and stand-up comedians use it to get laughs.

You've seen in the previous parts of this book that most laughs happen because the brain is surprised, triggered, or has been mind-bended. These things are usually easier to do in a conversation, because the speaker usually speaks fast and the listener's sound processing is good, so the brain is easily led.

That's why the funny effect will be much less when you write down a story that made people laugh, compared to when you tell it on stage or in conversation.

The good news?

Anything is possible, it's all about the method. When writing, instead of trying to get laughs by quickly triggering strong reactions like in conversation or telling jokes, where the brain is very "predictable" while reading, you can use a "safer" method.

This is also the secret that I and many of my writing course students have applied in many of our books, making readers enjoy them from beginning to end.

Let's see how this secret works in real life. The more your brain sees funny and vivid examples (and understands the principles behind them), the easier it will be for you to create similar examples of your own.

Understand the method through examples

1) Take Another Step

In my book *Vitasusu: 7 Super Effective Ways to Remember English Words*, there's a part where after talking about how hard I used to struggle reading books in foreign languages, I wrote:

Back then, I thought the reason was because of my "goldfish" brain. It wasn't just any kind of normal gold, it was shiny gold, maybe even pure gold!

This can be called the "take another step" technique, because normally people just say "goldfish brain" and that's it. I took another step, I analyzed the "level" of my brain's forgetfulness based on the color of the fish.

Then in my book The Prosperous Author, talking about a new path to help you write books faster and live a more free and happy life as an author, after sharing a memory of losing a large sum of money, I also applied this interesting technique and wrote:

There's a saying, "It never rains but it pours" meaning those who are already poor also face misfortune. I think the rain I got had turned into a storm that swept all my faith and hope away...

Do you see that?

From "rain" to "storm," from "pour" to "sweep" my hope away. If used wisely, this technique not only creates humorous vividness, but also expresses and connects deeper emotions.

Or one of my writing course students, she used this technique quite a bit to create word pictures when talking about heartbreak.

Heartbreak is not good for your "cardiovascular" health. However, there are some heart-boosting medications as follows:

Respect the other person's decision: Don't try to find answers to the unanswerable question "Why don't they like me?"

Maybe they don't even know the answer themselves...

You see, she not only compared "heartbreak" to a disease that affects the cardiovascular system, but also took another step by providing "heart medication."

2) Personifying Words

In my book 21 Guerrilla Ways For English Learners, I mentioned a tool to help you learn English effectively is to write a success journal: Simply list 5 small successes of the day each day. When sharing why readers should create this journal and try to be more creative, I wrote:

If you write 5 successes the same way every day, Mr. Success might not smile, but he might... smirk.

The brain always likes new things, so this habit will encourage you to think of things to do...

You see?

Mr. "Success."

Smiling and smirking...

That's also a pun. I not only personified an abstract word, but also "took another step" by talking about the types of smiles Mr. Success might give you.

3) Giving a New Name

In the book Befriend Your Emotions, Master Your Happiness by me and a co-author, you can find many passages where I played with words and used funny metaphors.

Here's an excerpt from the first chapter:

How to be happy?

At that time, 30 years of my life flashed before me like a movie, and the trailer was a distant memory when I was home alone and discovered two nostrils of a witch.

Actually, it was an electrical outlet, but for a curious kid, the fact that it could make the light bulb die and come back to life, or the fan spin, was truly magical. Maybe it would activate some kind of supernatural power in me?

Luckily, the two electrical outlet holes were too small for my toes, so I'm still alive!

I call this the "giving a new name" technique, which means you create funny names to spark curiosity for things that are simple and familiar to everyone.

Not only in textbooks, experience-sharing books, but you can also apply it in storybooks, novels.

If you open my book Light On, the first chapter, The Eagle Constellation, you'll see a passage where I wrote about Nata's thoughts about her mischievous brother Napa:

Napa stared at Nata's discovery as if it were the first time he knew about the existence of the number 57. Suddenly, Nata remembered that Napa was blind to numbers. He had struggled to graduate from kindergarten. Simply counting from one to ten was a miracle to him.

The little girl came up with a new term to describe her brother's condition: "number blind." A concept developed from "illiteracy." This example also has the element of "taking another step."

4) Exaggerating comparisons

You remember the story I told about my special superpower?

I didn't know that I have such a weird "superpower": Tell a joke and shut people up.

It's also a way of exaggerating comparisons, often starting with phrases like "as if...", "like..." accompanied by your unlimited imagination.

Or I also compared the doubts, the mocking laughter of people towards my dreams to what? That's right, bricks.

If you read all of my books (or reread them), you'll see that wherever I have the opportunity, I use these "wordplay" tactics quite flexibly!

Practicing Word-playing

The fun thing about this secret is that you don't have to set up and punch like the secrets in the previous section.

Why?

Because the goal is not to make readers laugh, but to stimulate the brain with interesting associative comparisons, and whether or not they laugh is a consequence.

That's why I say this technique is quite safe and used by most writers in their books. I often share with my writing course students that:

> Dry theory makes readers thirsty.

Therefore, you will see this technique in most of my books, and many of my writing students are also trying to apply it.

For example, one of my students applied this technique brilliantly when she recounted her experience of going to Singapore to be a manager, but ended up just being a lowly employee, listening to the boss's scolding every day.

"*I kick you home!*"

That's the yell I remember from my boss, a big fat man. His English grammar was all wrong but he still threatened me, with a contemptuous look in his eyes.

Kick me back to Vietnam? I wish he had actually done that, then I wouldn't have had to spend money on a return ticket.

In the above passage, she brilliantly played on the word "kick" to create a humorous and interesting perspective on her unforgettable painful experience.

I'm not going to hide it from you, this is a very flexible technique, and there is no general formula, so there is no way to practice it directly. So, I showed you a lot of examples in the previous section, with a total of 4 different ways to use it like that.

Summary of 4 Word-playing Techniques

1) The "Taking Another Step" Technique

Don't stop at common words (goldfish brain), go further (pure-gold or whale brain, for example).

2) The Personification Technique

Let abstract nouns speak for themselves by adding "Mr.", "Ms.", etc. in front of them. The God of Humor loves this.

3) The "Giving a New Name" Technique

Giving new names to old and common things,will help stimulate people's brains.

4) The Exaggerated Comparison Technique

Don't be afraid to use this technique multiple times, if you read Harry Potter, you'll see J.K. Rowling uses this technique a lot.

To have some top-notch "wordplay" kungfu, or unique exaggerated associations, you can practice them indirectly through these two skills:

1) Language Training

2) Creativity Training

Many people believe that the above two things mostly come from talent. Maybe, but I believe that to master them, it's mostly due to hard work.

Language training

Since 2012, I've been reading and posting inspiring quotes on my Facebook almost every day.

This not only helped me get over 40,000 followers on my Vietnamese Fanpage "Fususu" (with zero advertising), but also significantly improved my language skills.

At the same time, I created the legendary Treasure Chest product, which includes hundreds of inspiring quotes with impressive wordplay, and has sold thousands of sets.

You can view these images completely free of charge to train your language thinking. Simply scan the QR code below, and you can receive an interesting image via Messenger every day (with English subtitle)

leorowan.com/qrhumor5

Here are some suggestions

1) Find and read inspiring quotes

Quotes, poems, even song lyrics are not only rich in imagery, but often rhyme as well. Read them carefully and pay attention to how the author "dances" with their words.

2) Play language games

Solving crosswords, or language-related riddles, especially word-guessing games, will help you have a good time while training your language brain.

3) Re-read your favorite books

The first time you read, you usually just read for entertainment. But when you re-read,

read multiple times, and pay attention to the author's use of language, you are giving your brain a great learning opportunity.

4) Try learning a programming language

Although programming is not directly related to natural language, it also requires logical and structural thinking.

You can try learning a simple programming language with high applicability like HTML, Javascript, which can help you create your own website later.

5) Be bold and share your opinions in discussions

Group discussions on a topic are a great opportunity for you to use your vocabulary to express your opinions. Through this, you will not only become more confident in expressing your opinions, but you can also use language more flexibly.

6) Practice translation

You can choose a quote, a book excerpt you like, or a song in a language that is not your native language, to translate, then compare it to other translations.

This will not only help you expand your vocabulary, but also help you understand more about language structure and how to use language flexibly to express the same idea.

Creativity Training

There are many ways to train your creativity, like playing creative thinking games, doing new things every day, and so on. Personally, I believe that the fastest (and most fun) way is to develop your super memory.

It sounds strange, how is memory related to creativity?

Because simply to remember quickly and for a long time, you need to create unique, new, and impressive connections for your brain.

For example, walking down the street and seeing a license plate number 3656, immediately in my mind will appear two images from the Numagician book: the pig 36 and the life buoy 56.

Right after that, I'll try to find a connection between these two images and create a vivid image. For example, a pig swimming with a life buoy, or more creatively, I'm swimming with a pig-shaped life buoy.

By doing this, I not only remember the number right away, but also stimulate my creativity every day. And honestly, sometimes the new images I create on the road have made me laugh with joy!

This is just a small application in the Numagician book, which helps you train your memory through numbers, and then use them to remember everything in life with the memory hook method.

After a period of training, especially participating in the journey to conquer

Mount Pi at the end of the book, it would be strange if your creativity doesn't "level up."

One stone hits three birds, you will:

- ★ Be more creative
- ★ Remember better
- ★ Be funnier

Try it now!

One important note:

If you have trouble creating funny and creative stories, it doesn't mean you're not talented. It's simply because your brain hasn't been exposed to enough funny and creative connections like that.

Therefore, the simplest way is to practice more, or even simpler, read a lot of children's stories, where anything can happen.

That's also why, besides writing books to share skills for adults, I also write quite a few funny story books:

- Light On: A novel about a little girl who takes medicine to sleep well, but wakes up in another world.
- Short story collection about numbers: Numagician - The Magic Numbers And Untold Stories.
- Super short story collection about numbers: Numagician - Awake The Creative Artist Within
- Short story collection about letters: Almagician - The Story Of Magic Letters

You might think, "This technique only applies to writing, right?"

Not really, when you practice enough, you can flexibly apply word-playing in communication and presentations!

The Nail and the Hammer

I remember at a Toastmasters club meeting in Da Nang, I was the evaluator for a woman who had to give a prepared speech.

She had a very good presentation with a very clear structure of 4 main points, and I especially noticed that each point she made was accompanied by a very vivid example. Sometimes it was a story, sometimes it was a quote, sometimes it was a question, sometimes it was a unique experience.

Then it was my turn, you know how I started my evaluation?

"Do you know Thor?" I said. "The powerful guy in Marvel movies with the big hammer. I think today we've met... his wife."

(Everyone laughed and didn't understand why).

I continued, "If you compare each message to a nail, and the accompanying illustration to a hammer, then today our speaker has been outstanding. She has successfully hammered 4 message nails into our heads. Do you remember what they are?"

Then the audience nodded and repeated the 4 main points of the speech accurately. And of course, humor brings success, that day I won the award for best evaluator.

KEY #6
PREPARED RESPONSES

Have you ever planned to present something, but everything went differently than you expected? What would you do then?

For example, when preparing the introduction for a speech about writing books, I planned to say:

"*Let's start with a riddle. Where do you think there are the most amazing books, but they've never been published?*"

The plan was for the audience to share some ideas, then I would give the answer and explain, leading into my speech.

"*Thank you for your ideas, my answer is... the graveyard, because...*"

Everything would be perfect if the plan went according to script. However, what if the audience stays silent after you ask the question? Or what if someone says the answer you already prepared?

If there's one thing I've learned from champion speakers, it's the power of preparation.

Prepared minds, ready smiles!

Champion speakers are always prepared for anything that might happen. They make it part of their talk, even creating some laughs. This secret helps them not only feel more confident, but also makes their talk feel more natural.

For example, in the situation above, I would anticipate the possible situations and think ahead about how to respond.

1) If the audience is silent, I would say:

"Such a quiet atmosphere. Maybe the answer gave you chills. Yes, the answer is... the graveyard. Why?"

2) If someone says the answer I prepared, "the graveyard," I would say:

"That's great! How did you know? Did you dig up some book out there? (audience laughs) Yes, that's right. Why?"

3) What about a different answer?

If the audience gives different answers, I would thank them, ask for applause, and continue my talk as planned.

Especially if the audience gives unusual answers (that are funny), I would make a note of it. For my next presentation, I could liven things up by sharing the funny answer from before.

Then, you can imagine the next presentation starting like this:

"Let's start with a riddle," I say. "Where do you think there are the most amazing books, but they've never been published?"

"The publishing house?" an audience member says.

"That's true," I reply. "It's true that there are quite a few manuscripts in the warehouses of publishing houses that haven't been reviewed. Anything else?"

(the audience is silent)

I continue, "Last time, someone even said the answer was... under his bed."

(the audience laughs)

"Oh," I explain. "It's because he found a bunch of old love letters from his dad to his mom in there."

(the audience laughs even louder)

You see, the power of preparation is truly amazing, right?

You won't just make the audience laugh naturally, but you can also use the humor of situations that have happened before, contributed by the audience themselves, to help make your new speech richer.

Prepared Responses Strategy

This is a technique used in presentations to make things more interesting and get people laughing.

It's simple: for every question you ask, you need to have at least three answers ready:

1. ***What to say if no one answers:***

You can use an idea from a past talk or have a few ideas ready to use as examples.

2. ***What to say if someone answers correctly:***

Say "Thank you," give them a big clap, and say a funny comment you've already prepared.

3. ***What to say if someone has a different idea:***

Say "Thank you," clap, and laugh if their idea is funny. Or you can say something funny to respond to them if you can think of it right then.

Practice preparing your responses.

Imagine you're getting ready to give a speech and you're going to ask the questions below. Try to think about what might happen, and how you will respond, then compare your ideas with mine.

Remember: It's not easy to be funny when you're caught off guard. So, the main goal is to feel confident answering, and if you get a laugh, that's great! If not, that's okay too.

1) Presentation on Psychology

Question: "What do you think about people who always say they can't live without their smartphones?"

If they are silent, what would you say?

Leo: "Too quiet, maybe they're texting someone right now!"

If they agree with you, what would you say?

Leo: "What are they texting? 'Hey smartphone, how are you today?'"

If they have a different idea, what would you say? For example, they say, "Oh, it's my wife!"

Leo: "Congratulations, because your wife hasn't decided to marry a phone yet."

2) Speech about Art

Question: "Do you think Picasso is the greatest artist of all time?"

If they are silent, what would you say?

Leo: "Maybe they're lost in admiring Picasso's paintings! And I wonder if this scene of me standing on stage is in one of his paintings."

What about when the audience agrees?

Leo: "Awesome, we can open a Picasso gallery right here!"

If they have a different idea, what would you say? For example, they say, "No, I think... my dad!"

Leo: "Congratulations, next time bring your dad's paintings here, we can hold an auction."

3) Speech about Technology

Question: "Are you worried that AI will replace humans in the future?"

If they are silent, what would you say?

Leo: "Wow, many eyes are looking at me like they want to ask: Is the person speaking here an AI?"

What about when the audience agrees?

Leo: "If it happens, that's great. We'll retire early, right?"

If they have a different idea, what would you say? For example, they say, "No way!"

Leo: "Right. Actually, AI won't be able to replace those who can't be replaced. Who are they?"

4) Speech about Business

Question: "Do you think customers are always right?"

If they are silent, what would you say?

Leo: "Maybe you're thinking about the times when you weren't right?"

What about when the audience agrees?

Leo: "Awesome, we can open a business with customers as CEOs, and it will always grow!"

If they have a different idea, what would you say? For example, they say, "No, I'm."

Leo: "So, we probably need to open a company where you are the customer."

5) Speech about Cooking

Question: "Do you think cooking is a form of art?"

If they are silent, what would you say?

Leo: "Some of you are looking at me like you're wondering: Does instant noodles count as cooking?"

What about when the audience agrees?

Leo: "Awesome, it seems like we have a lot of artists here."

If they have a different idea, what would you say? For example, they say, "Not really..."

Leo: "Exactly. I think cooking is only art when the cook is an artist, but I can't guarantee the opposite..."

6) Speech about Sports

Question: "Do you think sports are a good way to build teamwork?"

If they are silent, what would you say?

Leo: "Maybe you're busy thinking about the times you played soccer and no one passed the ball to you?"

What about when the audience agrees?

Leo: "Awesome, you guys are really united. Maybe sitting in the office and typing together is a sport too?"

If they have a different idea, what would you say? For example, they say, "It depends on the sport..."

Leo: "Oh, are there any sports that decrease teamwork?"

7) Speech about Nutrition

Question: "Do you think eating vegan can help improve health?"

If they are silent, what would you say?

Leo: "Maybe many people are thinking about how much of their dinner last night was vegetables..."

What about when the audience agrees?

Leo: "That makes me always wonder why when I was sick, everyone told me to eat meat to get healthy?"

If they have a different idea, what would you say? For example, they say, "Tigers eat meat, they are super healthy!"

Leo: "Yes, that's right. But what do you think about animals that are stronger than tigers like buffalo, cows, elephants, what do they eat?"

You see, the key to this natural humor secret is interacting with the audience. The best way to get good at it is to practice as much as possible.

- ❖ What are you going to ask your audience in your next presentation?
- ❖ What are some answers they might give?
- ❖ How are you going to reply to each answer in a funny way?

The more you prepare, the more confident you'll be, and everything will go smoothly.

You might think, "But I don't have many opportunities to be on stage like that."

Then you can create your own stage at home, with you as the audience. And on the screen is one of your speeches.

Then, get some popcorn and enjoy your own video speech recordings!

Then, pay attention to the parts where you ask the audience, and someone in the audience might have said something cool, but we usually don't notice because we're too busy talking. Trust me, if you record your speech, you'll find a treasure trove of humor!

But anyway, having a positive practice environment is still the most effective. I recommend you check out Toastmasters International. I myself have founded 3 Toastmasters clubs in Vietnam to help me and my club members practice our skills and "polish" the stories we want to tell.

Keep practicing, and you'll not only make your presentation more engaging, but your audience will also find your speech unique, natural, and as if it were just for them!

What about writing?

If you think of each article as a conversation with your readers, you can use this trick to create engaging introductions.

For example:

What makes a man?

His intelligence?

The distance from his head to the sky?

The answer: his parents.

See, life is simple, we don't need to complicate things...

Another example:

What would you do if you found a million dollars?

Where would you travel?

What would you buy?

Actually, the first thing you should do is call the police, or you'll have trouble later.

See, sometimes we want to do what we want, but we forget the important things we need to do... let's explore the topic "The Art of Decision Making: Distinguishing Between Wants and Needs."

If you pay attention, you'll see that this is also an application of the "set-up-punch" principle from before, or you can call it something else like "surprised lead-in."

It's simple, you ask a question, give some answers yourself, and the third answer is usually a surprise. Then, you lead into the topic you want to talk about.

You might think, "Oh, that's too hard! How can I come up with cool answers?"

Don't worry, you don't have to be super clever to be "cool," you can follow these 3 simple steps.

3 Steps to Surprise Lead-Ins

If you look closely at the two examples above, you'll see that the answers are actually very simple. The humor is created by the two previous sentences, making your brain think about something more serious.

Step #1) Choose a simple question.

Example: What color is the sky?

Step #2) Give at least 2 unusual answers.

If you say the sky is blue, I think you're a positive optimist.

If you say black, I think you like the mystery of the night.

Step #3) Give a simple answer.

Actually, the sky has no color.

In this chapter, we'll discuss the topic of "optimism or reality."

Try practicing these 3 steps and compare your answers to mine!

Practice Surprise Lead-Ins

For each question below, try to think of 2 answers that are high-minded, complex, dreamy, or unusual... and the third answer should be as simple as possible. Then lead into a related topic.

After you read the question and do it yourself, you can compare your answers to mine. Or if you don't find my answers very funny, try to see if you can make them funnier!

1) How many hours are there in a day?

If you are very happy, the answer could be 12 hours.

If you are very sad, the answer could be 36, or even 72 hours.

The answer is 24 hours, because whether you are sad or happy, time still goes by. So instead of managing time, learn how to manage your emotions...

2) What would you do if you knew exactly the day you would die?

You would live every remaining moment to the fullest and finish your unfinished dreams.

Or spend time with your family, cherish the little things in life.

Why doesn't anyone think about... Buying a lot of life insurance?

And when you leave, the people left behind will cry, then smile brightly at the huge fortune you leave them. Yes, today we will talk about the topic "The art of leaving a legacy"...

3) Why does the sun rise in the east?

Is it because God's house is in that direction?

Or because if the sun rose from the west, people would have to change millions of textbooks, and that would be very expensive?

In fact, the sun rises in the east because of the Earth's rotation and the planet's rotation.

You see, sometimes the problem is not with the object that creates the problem, but with how we perceive it...

4) How to manage emotions well?

Maybe you are thinking of high-level principles...

Maybe you are thinking of meditation techniques...

Actually, no one likes to be managed. Emotions are the same. Today, let's learn how to be friends with our emotions...

5) Someone cute says they will give you their heart, how would you react?

Would you feel shy and not know what to say?

Do you feel great and would give them your heart back?

Wait, what would a heart surgeon say about this?

Today, we will learn about the function and real role of the heart.

6) Why does someone laugh when you smile at them?

Could it be because they are friendly?

Or because it is a habit of humans, scientifically proven.

Answer: Maybe you have something stuck in your teeth.

Yes, today we will learn about oral health.

7) If you were allowed to bring one item to heaven, what would you choose?

A family photo to always be reminded of the people you love?

Or a diary to help you remember what happened?

I like airplanes, so I can fly home. Today we will discuss the topic: Fantasy and reality.

KEY #7
LEARN AND LAUGH

How to Get Over Pain

That time I had a backache, so I decided to go for acupuncture. When I got there, the shop was closed. Following a friend's suggestion, I went to a massage place run by blind people.

After stepping out of the steam room, I felt very relaxed. A massage therapist was waiting for me.

"Do you want it strong or light?" he asked.

"Whatever," I replied. "As long as you feel it's best."

If you were there with me, you wouldn't just smell the soothing lemongrass oil, but also hear the calming background music, in complete contrast to the scene of the massage therapist jumping on me and starting to stomp. Feeling like my insides were going to burst, I was about to scream, but thinking that this was probably the "best" way, I gritted my teeth and endured. Finally, I survived 60 minutes, with... my whole body aching.

"How is it?" my friend asked. "Is your backache gone?"

I nodded and said, "Today I learned a way to get over pain without having to face it."

"What way?"

"Well, it's finding a bigger pain."

My friend burst out laughing.

It's true that at that time, my backache was completely overshadowed by the pain all over my body. But I still laughed because of the interesting lesson that the massage therapist had taught me about how to get over pain.

The next day I woke up feeling incredibly refreshed...

Keeping the Spirit of Humor

You know what the coolest thing is about being a public speaker or an author like me?

Becoming famous?

Being loved by many people?

For me, it's this: Every bad luck can become a cool story!

If something doesn't go your way, you might think it's bad luck. But champion speakers see it as an opportunity to discover themselves, a gold mine to dig for humor. They embrace it with a positive attitude and turn it into a cool story on stage.

As for a 5-star author, they see it as a treasure. For them, every pain is an asset, helping them make money, helping them "give birth" to many great chapters later.

Like a student in my writing course once wrote:

I'm happy that right now, my life and my ex-husband's life are both going in a positive direction. My ex, he's found joy in his new marriage. And I've found love with myself. The mark of the wedding ring on my finger has healed without me knowing. And the scar in my heart from that time has now become meaningful pages in my book (let's laugh together).

I realize: Pain heals with time, but it will definitely leave a lasting scar. Change your perspective: "It's a beautiful tattoo, and because of it, I'll be strong."

Or another student in my writing course once wrote:

With those good achievements, I was excited to enter the university entrance exam. I diligently studied all night and day like a soldier determined to defend the last stronghold, where the hopes of my loved ones are stored...

In those 3 days of the exam, I gave it my all. I felt like a pioneering knight on an invincible iron horse, charging into battle...

And you know what, I fell off the horse.

It was a painful memory for her, but with her lively writing style, she not only healed herself, but also created excitement for readers to adventure through her helpful book.

Human nature is to always find ways to avoid pain and seek comfort. Therefore, people are often stimulated, even very excited about the tragedies... of others.

Movie studios and television stations also use this as a motivation to grab the attention of viewers. They always want viewers to sigh in relief after watching, "Thank goodness it didn't happen to me!"

However, I don't encourage you to do silly things to "find things" to tell people. I'm not responsible if you've tried to "hunt for bad luck" like that!

Instead, simply get into the habit of finding positive meaning (even humorous) for the things that haven't gone your way. From there, you draw a useful lesson, or some way to make others laugh when you're asked about it.

This is the spirit of "learn and laugh," meaning that you yourself must find the things that happen to you—no matter how bad they are—funny in some way. If you find yourself laughing when you think back on something, chances are your audience will find it funny too.

How to Stay Positive?

What do you see in the picture below?

If you see a sad boy, try flipping the book over. You'll see something amazing!

Do you see a smiling boy?

It's the same with every event in life. Depending on what you focus on, your mind will have corresponding associations, creating emotions that guide your actions.

The story goes that there was a troop of soldiers who fell into an enemy ambush. They were surrounded on all sides, with no way to escape. The deputy general went to the general for advice.

"Sir," the deputy general said. "The morale of the troops is low, we're going to lose!"

The general went out and shouted, "Brothers, now the enemy is all around us, which means every bullet you fire will surely hit. Use all your firepower!"

Hearing 'every bullet will surely hit', the soldiers laughed, their fighting spirit overflowing.

Finally, the troop broke through the siege, and the general was increasingly trusted for his positive optimism.

With every event that happens, you can be like the deputy general, looking at the sad side and becoming pessimistic, or like the general, looking at the smiling side and becoming optimistic and positive.

Recently, I published a small journal called "Vipassana Massage Diary," about my time in a 10-day Vipassana meditation retreat. I remember that night, my wife read it and giggled from beginning to end, and decided to go meditate with me.

"What are you laughing at?" I asked.

"Oh, lots of things..." my wife said. "The part about changing 36 sitting positions and still having sore legs, and how you came up with different strategies to count leaves..."

Remembering that, I also burst out laughing. I'm sharing a passage here so you can see my "humorous" spirit in that moment at the meditation retreat, when I had to wait for too long. Normally people might get upset, but guess what I did?

Excerpt from "Vipassana Massage Diary"

I couldn't let time pass by uselessly, and sitting outside to meditate wasn't a good idea either. I decided to challenge my brain by... counting leaves.

Even though I knew I might transition from the "counting leaves" stage to "picking up leaves", and finally become crazy, I couldn't stop dreaming about this idea.

Oh, what are some ways to count leaves on a tree?

I came up with all sorts of tricks to count them.

Maybe we can do it as a team, the more people the better, each person picks a few and then counts, we'll get it done somehow?

That would be too labor-intensive, or maybe we can use paint to brush on one leaf and measure the volume of paint used, then use a fire hose to spray the whole tree, then take the total volume of paint, divide it by the volume used on one leaf?

Doing that, I might have to contact the fire department, and I can't tell them that there's a tree on fire, I need them to spray paint, not water. They might send me to a mental hospital before the leaf-counting project is complete.

Or maybe we can shake the tree really hard so all the leaves fall off, then gather them all into... a money counter?

Finally, the idea I liked best was to call my best friend and proudly announce that I can talk to the tree spirit and just say a random number, like 2500 leaves.

When he asks, "Is there really a tree spirit?" I'll reply, "If you don't believe it, count it yourself."

And that's how... the problem is solved completely!

There are many more interesting passages in the diary. If I ever translate the whole diary, you should read it and see how I maintained my "humorous" spirit in those 10 special days of pain and ache.

Start Your Humorous Diary

Start building your own "Humorous Diary" today!

Simply write down every memorable moment in your life, especially the things you want to forget:

- ★ What are the worst things that have ever happened to you?
- ★ Looking back now, what positive lessons have you learned?
- ★ Is there anything that, when you change your perspective, can be funny?

Trust me, no matter what happens to you, it can all become a treasure trove of laughter, not only healing you, but also bringing joy to others.

This is also how I usually train authors, helping them turn their pain into captivating chapters, into valuable treasures of lessons. Not only does it help them heal themselves, but it also makes their readers remember it forever.

Develop the habit of responding positively in every situation and excavating humor in every memory you've experienced, you'll have abundant material for your speeches, and at the same time make your life more enjoyable and positive.

Unlocking Your Talent

Since practicing the exercises in this book, my brain has been popping out humorous ideas all the time.

At a Danang Toastmasters Club meeting, I *noticed something special: four people went over their time, all by more than four minutes.* So, *when* I *went on stage as a general evaluator,* I *said:*

"*Today's meeting reminds me of the movie Fantastic Four, because we have four superheroes who went over time.*"

The whole room burst into laughter and started paying attention to my speech from beginning to end.

Many people believe that there is a fear worse than death, which is the fear of public speaking. I believe that there is something even scarier than speaking in front of a normal crowd, which is impromptu speaking (without any preparation).

Then, at a Hue Toastmasters Club meeting, I was invited to speak in a table topic session. That means you don't get any preparation, you have to speak right after you get the topic.

That day, they gave me a pretty difficult situation: "When your mother is silent, just busy cooking and doing housework."

The slide simply said that, no other suggestions. Normally, I might freeze, but for some reason, I started my speech very confidently:

"Have you ever made your parents upset?"

When parents are upset, they can yell and scream, but sometimes they can be so sad that they don't want to say anything, swallowing their tears...

(Everyone started commenting and liking the post below...)

Honestly, I'*ve always been a good kid,* so *if my mom is quiet, busy* cooking *and doing housework without saying anything all day,* it *can only be because she... has a sore throat.*

(The guys below burst into laughter non-stop)

After that, I continued my speech and ended with a meaningful message: Sometimes parents don't say anything, it doesn't mean they don't love us, let's understand them.

The speech beat out over 7 other impromptu speakers and won first place in impromptu speaking that day. It's a prize I rarely win even though I have a lot of experience speaking (because I usually give prepared speeches, I'm really scared of this Table Topic part).

Personally, at this point, when I think back, I can't help but laugh at the idea of "mom having a sore throat."

Not only in Toastmasters, this often happens in my wife and I's life. Sometimes, I often say things that make my wife laugh happily.

For example, one time my wife was scrolling through Facebook and I was shaving. Facebook suddenly showed an ad for permanent hair removal. So I said, "Oh, why does Facebook understand me so much..."

My wife burst out laughing.

You see, all of the above situations, my funny comments came out unexpectedly, I didn't prepare anything at all.

I'm really surprised because my brain's ability to connect after a period of training has become so quick. Talent, after all, is just a kind of reflex, formed by connections in the brain. When activated, the brain will automatically do what it's been trained to do without you having to think.

Because I've been practicing "wordplay" regularly, creating good sentences, and combining it with frequent writing, my language skill has taken a big step forward, from the time I got a bad score on my elementary school graduation literature exam, to the time I published over 20 books...

That helped me quickly "give wings" to words, create comparisons, and vivid metaphors. Combined with the habit of regular creative training through memory exercises, my brain has the ability to connect very quickly and automatically provide interesting suggestions, or unexpected "turns."

If you can do that, you'll easily guide people's emotions from sadness to joy, making them unable to take their eyes off your speeches on stage, and unable to leave their screens during online speeches.

Just be persistent, practice the right way, and one day you'll be surprised by yourself when someone comes up to you and says:

"Oh, you're so charming when you talk!"

"Wow, you're so funny, I couldn't stop laughing when I heard you talk. What's your secret?"

(At that point you can introduce them to this book, so you don't have to explain much)

FAREWELL GIFT

Thanks for choosing this book, and especially for reading this far!

Let’s make a big smile, as a reward for yourself. As far as I know, nowadays, besides textbooks at school that are required to read, most people don't read books like this, let alone finish them!

If you haven't read from the beginning and have skipped to here, then smile even brighter. Because you can grasp all the important knowledge of the book, just after reading the last chapter.

Of course, just "knowing" without practicing, it will be difficult to help you develop a "sense of humor". Therefore, whether you have read from the beginning or skipped to the end, I still hope you read this book many times and find ways to practice whenever possible. Before parting ways with a gift of inspiration, let's summarize the 7 important things I want to share with you through this book.

7 Things to Keep in Mind

1) Don't Try to Be Funny

Don't try to be funny by telling jokes you've collected, but dig up laughter from your own real stories. That humorous treasure will help you always be yourself, while still being funny and charming.

2) Always Go One Step Further

Humorous treasure is not only hidden in the dialogue or reactions of the characters in the story, but also in their possible thoughts (or yours now when looking back at that story). Go beyond ordinary storytellers, pay attention to small details, and you'll find the treasure of laughter always there.

3) Know the General Rules, But Be Flexible in Applying Them

There may be a few general rules for humor like set-up-punch... but honestly, there are no limits, creativity is entirely up to you. The simplest trick to becoming more creative is to master the general rules and apply them a lot.

4) Don't Try to Make People Laugh

Instead, make their brains surprised. Then, laughter is often just a consequence. Read a lot of examples, try to master the setup-punchline, mind-bending tricks. Once they get into your blood, your brain will often come up with humorous ideas on its own, and you'll be surprised yourself.

5) All Languages Are Rich and Beautiful

Often, humor comes from using vivid language. Play around with words often, and naturally the god of Humor will often smile at you, while you are happy to bring laughter to everyone.

6) Often, Humor is Due to Preparation

Most comedians have thorough preparation before going on stage. Like a magic trick, often, the most natural-seeming humor comes from the most careful preparation.

You've been equipped with the "prepared responses" technique to make interacting with your audience more fun, apply it and make your presentation or writing more impressive and memorable.

7) Humor is Also a Skill

Humor, seemingly a talent, but actually it can be completely trained by combining: Language thinking, creativity, and a positive optimistic spirit. Persistently practice with the right method, you will reach your destination.

The Story of Oliver Fun

Once upon a time, in the forgotten land of Jolivia, there lived a boy named Oliver Fun. Even though he was born into a family famous for stand-up comedians, Oliver was very serious. The number of shooting stars in the night sky all week was probably more than the number of times he laughed... all year.

Oliver's parents were worried. This lack of humor not only made it hard for him to follow in his family's footsteps, but it could also make him miss one of life's greatest joys: laughter. So, when they heard about the Legendary Humor Training Camp—which promised to unlock the hidden laughter within everyone—they signed Oliver up right away.

When he arrived at the camp, Oliver was surrounded by laughter. The trainers were all professional comedians with different styles.

This made Oliver want to be funny too, but he thought: I'm not talented.

One trainer, with a white beard like a Santa Claus, said confidently, "Right now, everyone will tell a joke. Whoever makes everyone laugh the most wins!"

A cute girl said, "What does one wall say to another wall? Meet you at the corner!"

Everyone laughed their heads off.

A big guy said, "Why don't skeletons fight even after they come back to life? Because they don't have the guts."

Every time someone spoke, the whole camp burst into laughter, except for Oliver. He was too busy thinking about what he would say when it was his turn. He saw that everyone seemed to be great at thinking on their feet, but he couldn't think of anything.

"Oliver," the trainer said. "It's your turn!"

Oliver went silent, his breath quickened, his hands shook, his mouth felt like it was stuck with whale tape, he couldn't say a word.

Someone in the class yelled, "Do you need medicine for 'humor'?"

The whole camp had a good laugh.

Oliver felt incredibly embarrassed. He slumped down, trying to hide the tears that were about to spill.

Another student shouted, "His name is Oliver Fun, but he's not Fun at all, teacher!"

The whole camp laughed even louder.

Oliver couldn't take it anymore. He stood up and tried to run outside, but the trainer quickly caught him. The trainer's kind smile helped Oliver calm down.

The trainer signaled for everyone to be quiet and said, "Legendary humor doesn't come from making fun of others, it comes from a heart that knows how to laugh at ourselves.

Oliver, I haven't seen you smile all day. What's bothering you?"

Oliver wiped his tears and said, "Sir, I'm afraid I won't be able to make everyone laugh."

"Oh, don't worry. Just make yourself happy first. From the past, is there any memory that you found impressive?"

Oliver hesitated for a moment, then an idea popped into his head. "Oh, once when I was coming home from school, I saw a pan of golden fried rice. After I finished eating, I found out it wasn't fried rice, it was... spoiled rice. I was impressed because... I'm still alive!"

The whole camp burst into laughter, making Oliver gape in surprise. It was the first time he had made everyone laugh so much, and he still didn't understand why they were laughing.

The trainer tried to hold back his laughter and asked, "So what are you thinking now?"

"Sir," Oliver said. "I'm wondering if every time I want to make people laugh, I'll have to keep... eating spoiled rice?"

The whole camp erupted in laughter again, with many laughing so hard they fell to the floor, rolling around, clutching their stomachs. The trainer couldn't hold back his laughter this time.

Seeing this, Oliver was very worried. He blurted out, "But... my mom only knows how to cook cooked rice, I'll have to cook the spoiled rice myself, teacher!!!"

The trainer tried to cover his mouth. "Calm down, Oliver, it's not what you think..."

Then the trainer explained that everyone was laughing because of Oliver's current thoughts about the event, along with his innocent questions. Finally, he said, "Oliver, you have a natural talent for humor, keep practicing!"

Hearing this, Oliver was very happy. He followed the trainer's instructions: he wrote down all the events that had happened to him in the past, and then the whole camp paired up and shared their stories with each other.

The first person Oliver paired with was a girl. He told her about the time he was bitten by a dog, and ended with a question, "Like spider-man, could it be that after being bitten by a dog, we turn into dog-man?"

She laughed hysterically.

He kept pairing up with everyone, and Oliver made everyone laugh their heads off. The bad luck and sadness from his past seemed to have become a treasure trove of laughter within him.

On the last day of the course, the trainers and everyone gathered around Oliver, clapping and congratulating him on graduating with the highest honors.

Later, Oliver became the funniest person in Jolivia, and the pride of the Fun family. The stories Oliver told were all very real, and besides laughter, they also contained very profound lessons.

With sparkling eyes and a smile on his face, Oliver always ended his speeches with the legendary quote, "Laugh at others, you'll shorten your life. Laugh at yourself, you'll live longer (and happier)."

What did you learn from the story?

To be honest, even though I made up the story, every time I read it, I feel relaxed and learn new lessons about being naturally funny.

First, being naturally funny doesn't come from making fun of others, it comes from being confident, sincere, and able to see things in a positive way. Oliver learned to accept the imperfect things in his life and share them in a new way. That turned his memories into a treasure chest of real laughter.

Second, humor can be learned and developed. Oliver, although he didn't have a "talent" at first, when he was surrounded by funny people, and especially with the encouragement of a wise coach, his ability was awakened.

Third, did you notice that every time Oliver shared a story about himself, he not only made people laugh but also created a connection? Humor is a powerful tool to create connection, make us closer, understand each other better, and even create lasting relationships.

Let's apply these lessons, as well as the tips in this book, I'm sure we can become funnier, create deeper relationships, and live a happier life.

YOUR GIFT BOX

Wow, thanks for reading this far. I know becoming funny can change your life, but it's not always easy. If we think of presenting skills as different levels, here's how I see it:

★ Level 1: Confidently Presenting: You just dare to share your ideas.
★ Level 2: Clear Structure: You present in a clear and easy-to-understand way.
★ Level 3: Lively and Engaging: You create a powerful image in people's minds.
★ Level 4: Creating Good Feelings: You make them excited or touched.
★ Level 5: Impressive Humor: You make them laugh and remember it forever.

See? Humor is the highest level! To be honest, I, and this book, still have a lot to learn to fully understand the mystery of humor.

Recently, the whole world has been buzzing about artificial intelligence, with its ability to chat like a human, process text, and write smoothly. Everyone's praising it! But when I asked AI to rewrite funny paragraphs or tell jokes, I laughed because the concept of "humor" for humans and machines is completely different!

Nothing is perfect, right?

But I believe that by taking one step at a time, everything will be perfect. And on this journey, you're not alone. I'm always here for you, and other readers with the same goals are also ready to help. Scan the QR code to connect with me and the book's active reader groups. You'll also get 3 exciting books to help you on your journey.

leorowan.com/qrhumour6

Hope you always laugh,

Leo Rowan

(Signed from a beautiful beach)

P.s. Thanks again!

If you like the book, leave a review. Even a few words will make me smile all day.

Also, this is just the first version. You can send your ideas, especially funny examples you come up with to author@leorowan.com — If they fit, I'll include them in the book and acknowledge your contribution.

See you with a smile of success!

www.ingramcontent.com/pod-product-compliance
Lightning Source LLC
LaVergne TN
LVHW010102170826
845678LV00012B/2212

* 9 7 9 8 2 3 0 7 0 6 9 3 9 *